Contents

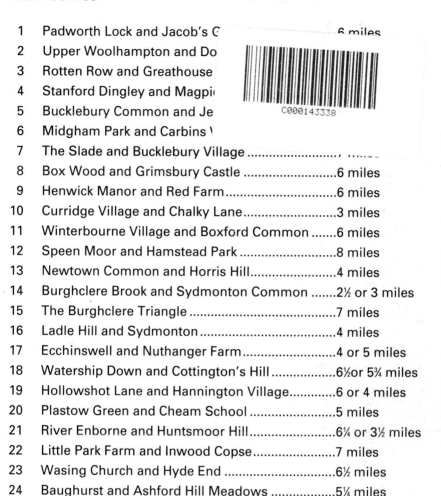

THE RAMBLERS' ASSOCIATION promotes country walking, protects rights of way, campaigns for access to open country, woodlands etc. and defends the beauty of the landscape. The RA plays a major role in securing legislation to protect our paths and countryside. Please give your support by becoming a member. Write to: The Ramblers' Association, 1/5 Wandsworth Road, London SW8 2XX, tel: 0171 582 6787.

BERKSHIRE AREA
The RA has four separate Groups in the County - West Berks, Mid Berks, South East Berks and East Berks. Each Group arranges its own extensive programme of walking and other events for a constantly growing membership. For details contact: Area Secretary, Mrs J Norris, 15 Southwold, Roman Wood, Bracknell, RG12 4XY.

Padworth Lock
and Jacob's Gully

This first walk is an opportunity to leave the car at home and to make it a 'rail ramble' (Sundays excepted). An especially rewarding walk in summertime, through wild flower-filled meadows; a typical stretch of peaceful Kennet Valley scenery, including Aldermaston Wharf, once a thriving centre of canal trade.

Distance: 6 miles
OS Maps: Pathfinder 1187 Newbury;
1188 Mortimer & Arborfield
Start: Aldermaston BR Station (Grid ref: 601674) See map for alternatives, such as A4 lay-by (666581)

From down-side platform 2 walk across car park, over road, through swing-gate and turn left along bank of Kennet & Avon Canal to lift-bridge at Aldermaston Wharf. Notice plaque recording the visit of HM The Queen in 1986.

Cross road (A340) and continue ahead along canal-side, passing 'British Waterways' Visitor Centre (canal-man's 200 year old cottage). At restored Padworth Lock carefully cross second lock-gate and follow path which soon turns right along an old 'haul route' between 1940s gravel pits, now 'reclaimed' by nature!

At junction turn left along tree-lined track (Mill Lane). Just beyond fish-farm shop turn right into tightly fenced path to cross series of Kennet River footbridges (have they something to hide at Padworth Mill?) to reach stile at field edge. Cross field ahead to footbridge and then go straight on (ignoring left fork) to stile on far side into woodland (Great Fishers). Cross bridge over culvert (worth a closer look) and follow climbing path to road, with refreshing-sounding Aqua Vitae Copse on right. Now turn right along lane, past saw-mill and idyllic Upper Church Farm. Opposite 'Ladywood' turn right over stile and free-wheel down right side of meadow, then along strip between fields, to pass right of secluded little artificial lake by Jacob's Gully.

About 30 yards beyond water's edge,

bear right to stile at field side. If path ahead is not apparent, set your sights on line of stately mid-field oaks, savouring the view across Kennet Valley as you climb. At fourth tree aim for stile in hedge, to left of power-line pole and in next field bear slightly right. After further stile bear left along fence to stile at road. Turn right along lane past stone gateway (Aldermaston Court) to reach open-fronted churchyard of St Mary-the-Virgin.

From churchyard cross road to enter field over stile and follow fence down, crossing three more stiles, to reach wide track (Fisherman's Lane). Here, turn left for 100 yards, then right, through gap in hedge, to go straight across three fields, with footbridges, to finally cross copse of poplars to reach road.

To shorten the walk, turn right over bridge and then first left, to reach Frouds Bridge, turning right along canal towpath and so back to Aldermaston Wharf.

To continue the full circuit, turn left and follow with care right-hand side of road ahead. Where this bears left, turn right through small parking area, cross a footbridge, turn left and shortly cross a further (wider) bridge, to join riverbank nearby on right. (Aldermaston Mill, now a hotel, is just down-stream.) With river on right, follow bank for about half mile to cross canal at Wickham Knights Bridge (built 1990 to replace a wooden swing-bridge here), returning along towpath on opposite bank. The next half mile brings you to Frouds Bridge where towpath crosses and we do too, to trundle the last leg back to the start.

One interesting point about the unlovely Sterling Cable works along here is that after the Great Western Railway acquired the canal in 1852, a basin was excavated on this site, linked to the lock, to facilitate transfer of goods between rail and canal.

DATE WALKED ☐ ☐ 19

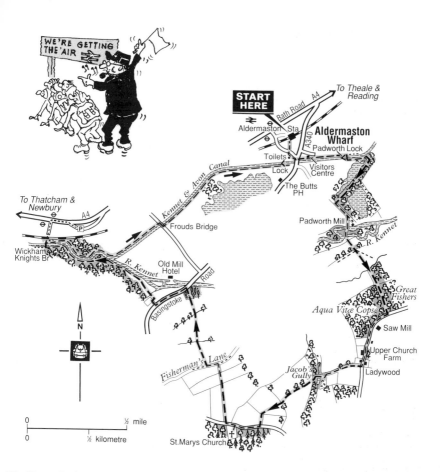

The Kennet & Avon Canal and towpath near Wickham Knights Bridge

Upper Woolhampton and Douai Abbey

Education and religion seem to thrive in the fresh air and fine scenery above Woolhampton. Our route links two venerable village churches with a modern abbey and two large schools.

Distance: 4½ miles
OS Map: Pathfinder 1187 Newbury
Start: Roadway by Elstree School, Upper Woolhampton. (Grid ref: 576675)

With back to school main entrance turn left along oak-lined road and at end of playing field turn right through swing-gate into broad grassy path. Pass pond on left and after bend cross two stiles, either side of woodland strip. Turn right along edge of field with copse on right and shortly after left-hand bend, turn right through gateway to enter Channel Wood, along broad track. At path junction bear right and shortly, at field entrance on right, enter field and follow headland path with woodland on left.

At top corner of field turn right still along wide grass track (look right for first glimpse of Douai Abbey). At end of field turn left, now with hedge on right and after stile by metal gate enter woodland strip, to emerge at roadside - Kiff Green. Turn right along road for about 100 yards and just beyond old farm buildings turn right over stile and through middle of paddock. After stile and footbridge,

reach and cross road ahead, entering field by stile. Follow hedge (and road) to right, leave field over stile, then turn left along wide headland with further views of Douai Abbey on right.

In 1903 the Benedictine Community of Douai, northern France, was expelled, returning to England after nearly 400 years. They came to what was then St Mary's College, Woolhampton, which they have developed into the prominent Catholic school it is today.

The Abbey Church was first consecrated in 1933 when the neo-Gothic sanctuary and choir were built, part of a massive design which was never completed. In 1987 architect Dr Michael Blee drew up plans for the nave and lantern to complete the structure in the contemporary style we see today. This building was consecrated in July 1993 and is open to visitors.

Continue on this path as it bears left into next field now with hedgerow and playing-field on right. At path junction go straight on into wood along gravel path and then between fences to reach lane at houses (Beenham). Turn right for 50 yards then left along tarmac path between properties, leading to play-area. Keep to right-hand edge of green and turn left along road.

St Mary's churchyard, Beenham

Look for narrow path on right, alongside garden fence of last terraced cottage and follow this over stile into field, passing buildings of Awbery's Farm to left. Follow stiles through next two meadows ahead with hedge on left until, just before end of second field, turn left over stile into woodland. Within a few yards reach drive. Here turn sharp right and follow verge to road (Back Lane). Now turn left and follow road round bend to take first turning right. (The 'Stocks' pub is a few yards left of junction.) Go 25 yards along Stoneyfield Road to bear left and where, after a few yards this track turns left, go straight on down narrow path, past bungalow on left, soon with open views across Kennet Valley, to emerge opposite lych-gate of St Mary's Church, Beenham.

Enjoy the views from this tranquil spot as you walk to left of porch and leave churchyard over stile in corner. Cross field on level path to enter wood (Old Copse) by stile and then down steep path. At end of woodland cross stile and turn left down wide gravel track. Follow left and right-hand bends then climb until, just before top of rise, turn sharp right up slope through gateway and

head half-left across field towards left-hand end of trees ahead. After stile by gate continue along side of next field before entering woodland by stile. Follow winding path to reach crossing track with open meadows ahead.

Taking a line slightly left, follow a series of squeeze-stiles through 3 paddocks to reach road in far corner. Turn right for 30 yards, then fork left over drive to reach playing-field. Follow edge with trees on left at first, then maintain same line through middle of field, soon with view of spire in trees ahead - St Peter's Church. Go through churchyard and turn left along road to return to start.

DATE WALKED | | | 19 |

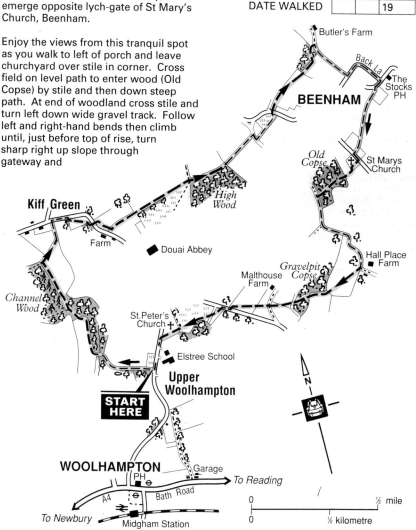

Rotten Row
and Greathouse Walk

This is truly a walk for all seasons but the well-wooded slopes of the Pang Valley make it especially rewarding in spring and autumn. Add to this the many tempting places to linger a-while and this becomes a walk to raise the spirits and lower the blood pressure!

Distance: 6 miles
OS Maps: Pathfinder 1171 Hermitage & Chieveley; 1172 Reading
Start: Rushall Manor Farm, off Back Lane, about 2 miles W of Bradfield. (Grid ref: 584723)

Near Stanford Dingley

Note: Walkers are welcome to park in this restored 700 year-old farmyard, by permission of the John Simonds Trust. The Trust aims to encourage young people's awareness of farming and love of the countryside. You may prefer to avoid some winter Saturdays when shooting takes place. Enquiries to John Bishop, tel: (01734) 744547.

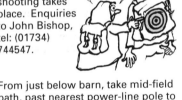

From just below barn, take mid-field path, past nearest power-line pole to stile at road (Back Lane). Turn right along lane and just before bottom of dip turn left, then immediately right over ditch, to cross narrow field (notice old well-head nearby on right). In next field follow hedge on right to bend in boundary, bear left across field straight towards church, crossing two small fields to reach St Denys's, a most uncommon saint.

Turn left through Stanford Dingley. Happiness is...an English village like this! At road junction turn left and after stile follow field fence to swing-gate, then along short length of wide track before crossing stile ahead and along left side of fields. Notice track on left by old watercress beds and Blue Pool, the latter caused by springs deep in the chalk here. Continue to end of field, go through swing-gate and shortly turn right over stile and climb to top left-hand corner of field and hamlet of Rotten Row.

Turn right up road by Slipper Cottage and after short steep climb, turn left between wooden rails along sunken path through Stanford Wood. Cross road, bearing left over stile and go straight ahead through several small paddocks to reach road (Mariners Lane). Now continue ahead through three bigger fields to cross drive between swing-gates. In next field notice solitary tree (small pine) on path ahead. Go 70 yards past it, then turn left to leave field over stile into narrow path, with fine views ahead over playing-fields of Bradfield College. Our way lies down steps and then slightly left to waymark post on far side of pitches, pointing to wooded banks of River Pang just ahead.

Turn right along this beautiful riverside path leading to cluster of old cottages, mill and church at centre of Bradfield. Turn left and follow road through village to crossroads. Here go half-left up steps in bank to take diagonal cross-field path, passing just to left of tree-screened pumping station. After two stiles ahead, with field between, path turns right, a few degrees away from hedge on right, to pass through gap in trees on boundary. Go diagonally through middle of next field to emerge through gap on stony track Great House Walk.

This steadily climbing bridleway passes Greathouse Cottage and then bears left, reservoir on right. Track descends (Broomhill Copse) and 60 yards beyond bottom dip, turn left along path through pines. A few blobs of white paint and remains of metal swing-gates help to indicate path line running straight ahead, finally to reach stile at field edge. Here

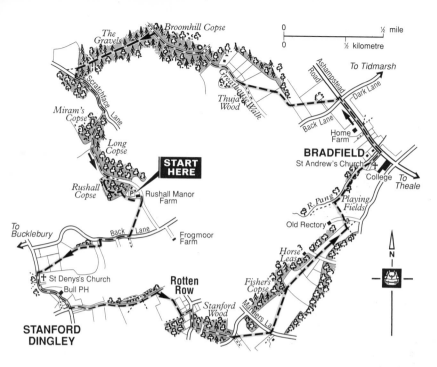

turn left and shortly left again along quaintly-named Scratchface Lane, a true delight in spring and autumn.

At end of field on right, bear right down stony path and soon continue on wide track with fine views across field on right. Look for Permitted Path on RIGHT

entering nature trail (Rushall Copse) and follow white marker-posts. At path junction in copse turn right, leading to edge of wood and follow new stony path back to start.

DATE WALKED | | 19

Bradfield church and college from our path across the playing fields

Stanford Dingley and Magpie Farm

This is an easy stroll up and down the slopes of the Pang valley. The tiny river may be low at times but liquid refreshment is never far away, with four old inns set conveniently into this fine tapestry of English countryside.

Distance: 7 miles
OS Maps: Pathfinder 1187 Newbury;
1171 Hermitage & Chieveley
Start: Blade Bone Inn, Chapel Row
(Grid ref: 571697)

From the 'Blade Bone' cross to village shop (why not treat yourself?). Turn left for a few paces, then right, signed to 'Bucklebury Village' along footway. After 150 yards turn right into hedged track. Where gravel surface ends continue on, with views opening up on right (notice line of Lombardy poplars). At end of enclosed path go through metal gate to follow left hand side of very long meadow until, just short of its end, leave through squeeze-way and continue along sunken track to road.

Halfway house

Here turn right to enter the delightful village of Stanford Dingley, passing 'Old Boot Inn' on right. Shortly, turn left along near side of the splendid Georgian 'Garden House' (note garden on opposite side of road) to cross mill stream (the modest River Pang), to reach road opposite 'The Bull'. Enjoy this unspoilt village street until, directly opposite the weather-boarded tower of St Denys's Church, turn left over stile and take diagonal cross-field path. On far side cross two stiles, with track between, to ascend headland with hedge on left.

At road turn left for 75 yards, then turn right to follow headland round two sides of field. At end of fence-line continue ahead between young trees along unfenced track towards buildings (Pangfield Farm). Reaching metal gate (before farm), follow new line of path by turning right for 50 paces, then left, eventually to join grass path along back of buildings. Now turn sharp right, through wooden gate, up rising sunken bridleway through light woodland, called rather inappropriately, Nightingale Green.

Where the well-used path turns left, go straight on through trees, soon to enter meadow by metal gate with open views ahead. Cross field to bridle-gate (see map for definitive line) and go half-left over next field towards woodland. Do not enter this wood but follow edge, keeping it on right. At end of wood cross stile, turn right for a few yards, then left through wire gate in deer fence. Cross this new plantation to exit at similar gate. Now follow wide grass path along left side of area of king-size Christmas trees. Path climbs gently to join track bearing left past well preserved buildings of Magpie Farm.

At top of drive cross lane and stile. Go ahead through three paddocks to enter woodland by stile and follow way-marked path along edge of Frilsham Common. Soon turn left on descending track leading to delightfully situated 'Pot Kiln' inn, with its spacious garden.

To continue, turn left along lane and where it bends left, turn right over stile to cross valley and enter woodland on far side. Follow rising path, over wide

THERSH FOUR PUBS ON THIS'H WALK HIC!

crossing track and after right-hand bend do not be tempted by prominent left-hand turn but go straight on through open woodland along grassy path. Where path begins steep descent look carefully for diverted path into trees on left, to follow route which soon descends steeply, with fence and field on right towards buildings of Rushdens Farm. Pass through paddocks to left of house to reach stile onto drive, turning left to road. Here cross carefully and go along sunken track leading to diminutive Pang which re-cross by footbridge a few yards left of ford. Take cross-field path away from river to stile in far hedge and continue in same direction through two more fields. Look back for fine views of valley as path climbs to reach stile at roadside.

Here turn left and, where lane bends, bear right, to left of 'Four Seasons' into narrow bridleway, rising in woodland with field on left at first. At top of climb (now Bucklebury Common) pass through garden of property on left and at start of drive just ahead, turn sharp left down bank and over ditch to pass pretty thatched cottage nestling below to left. Follow gravel drive and bear left at junction, along path beneath cables until the 'Old Bake House' (remember?) comes into view ahead, then bear right across Chapel Row Common to return to start.

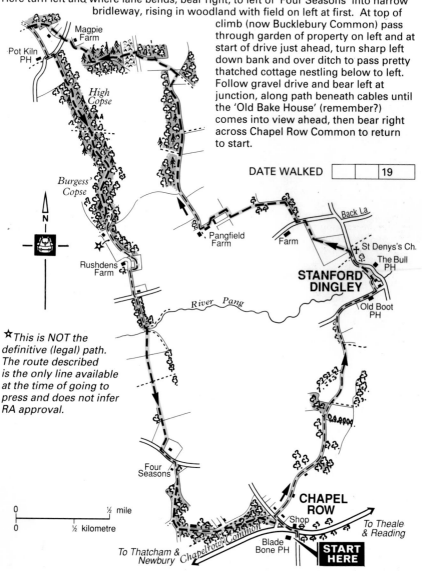

DATE WALKED [ ][ ][19]

☆ This is NOT the definitive (legal) path. The route described is the only line available at the time of going to press and does not infer RA approval.

Bucklebury Common and Jennettshill Wood

Bucklebury claims to have more footpaths than any other parish in England. The huge common also has more than its share of legends and ghostly sightings; two monks near the medieval fish-ponds we pass and a 'grisly apparition' said to appear in daylight at Bushnells Green. Don't be nervous - just walk a little faster in places!

Distance: 5½ miles
OS Maps: Pathfinder 1187 Newbury;
1171 Hermitage & Chieveley
Start: Blade Bone Inn, Chapel Row
(Grid ref: 571697)

From the 'Blade Bone' cross to village shop and turn left for a few paces to road junction. Cross road signed to 'Bucklebury Village' and head across the green, bisecting the two roads, passing to right of seat, into avenue of young trees. Soon bear left into wide strip, clear of trees. Now follow the power-line poles ahead (this is Chapel Row Common) for just over a mile (walk about 20 minutes) to reach third prominent crossing track. Turning right on this track and finding a single property just ahead on left will identify the correct route. Thirty yards beyond entrance to cottage (by large tree) bear right down path through bracken. Reaching fence ahead bear left, steeply downhill and pass to right of pond (one of a pair - see introduction). About 20 yards beyond pond bear right and enjoy views through trees.

Reaching road, turn right and at bottom of hill, just before cottage, turn left into bridleway through woodland with grassland (deer park) nearby on right. Reaching crossing track, turn right along tree-lined way with pleasant views. Just after secluded cottage 'Vanners' (a gateway onto the Common once stood here), bear right through double gates and then, within a few yards, enter the 60-acre Bucklebury Farm Park.

The path descends just to left of island copse (views ahead to village) to leave field in bottom corner at way-mark post pointing to track. Emerging from trees, pass through deer fence and head diagonally across grass, then over strawberry field (presently), aiming for cupola on farm buildings, to cross stile in hedge at roadside (Pease Hill). Turn left and shortly fork right past imposing Georgian house and buildings of Manor Farm.

Opposite last building on right (former school) bear left onto mid-field path along the broad flat bottom of Pang Valley (river is away to left). Continue ahead at path crossing, now with ditch on right. Cross plank bridge, turn right to corner of this field, then left along headland finally to reach road. Here turn right up lane and, at top of first rise, turn left along woodland bridleway (Bushnells Green). While not easy to follow in places, bear to left at far end, to leave corner of wood at metal bridle-gate. In open meadow ahead follow line of trees in gully to reach second metal gate. Continue along left side of next field until, facing a gate, turn right across field with ditch on left and cross stile leading to footbridge. Keep hedge on left in next field, then continue along enclosed path

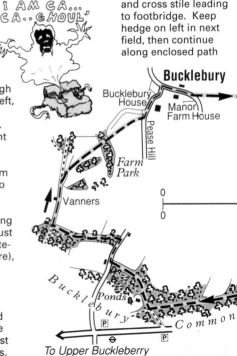

"I AM GA...
"GA..GHOUL"

Bucklebury

Bucklebury House

Manor Farm House

Pease Hill

Farm Park

Vanners

Bucklebury Ponds

Common

To Upper Buckleberry & Thatcham

Cottages at Chapel Row

to reach and turn left down road (Jennetts Hill).

At bottom of hill turn right and pass to left of Casey Court. Go between unlovely garage blocks to find stile. Cross field ahead to footbridge, then immediately turn right down bank and aim for gap in hedge, half-way up field boundary, onto path through small plantation. Turn left for just ten paces along track, then right, up increasingly steep path in Jennettshill Wood.

At top bear left past cottage, following drive to road (Bishops Road). Turn right to

T-junction, then right again (Cock Lane). Half-way round bend in road turn left through gate and across corner of field to exit by another swing-gate. Cross ahead into fenced path to right of nursery and reaching open Common go straight ahead along way-marked path. At crossing track, turn left for 15 yards, then fork right and soon right again, now with fields nearby on right. Shortly reach roadside edge of Bucklebury Common with its splendid row of oaks. Follow the oaks, on right at first, then cross over and continue back to start.

DATE WALKED [   ] [19]

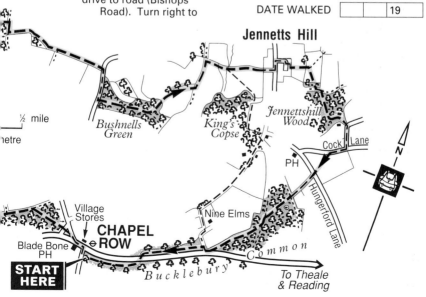

Midgham Park and Carbins Wood

An opportunity to discover a 'lost' path across the wild and heathery Bucklebury Common, to enjoy far-reaching views over the Kennet Valley and to stroll through the tranquil beauty of historic Midgham Park.

Distance: 3½ miles
OS Map: Pathfinder 1187 Newbury
Start: Limited off-road parking area
            on Lower Common, about 1
            mile NE of Upper Bucklebury
            (Grid ref: 560693)

From road walk 30 paces across gravel area, then bear right onto bridleway through fringe of trees. Maintain exactly same line over open common, keeping straight on at first crossing track. At next junction, again ignore paths to left and right, but carry on ahead now on byway, through trees at first. Reaching wide gravel track, cross this, as the right of way steers through the trees to road just ahead.

With care, cross road into tarmac drive between properties. Reaching entrance ahead to 'Wootens', go through swing-gate on right into enclosed path which provides fine views of the North Wessex Downs (AONB). Reaching a stile, go straight ahead down mid-field right of way to swing-gate at bottom corner. Turn right down this quiet lane, passing old school-house, until you reach Midgham's elegant Victorian church of St Matthew, worth visiting to enjoy unspoilt views across the fields of the Kennet Valley.

Leaving the churchyard, immediately turn right into gateway of West Lodge, the start of an almost mile-long path through the undisturbed meadows and rough grazing of Midgham Park.

The Manor of Midgham can be traced back to before the Norman Conquest and has several Royal connections. George II's second son, the Duke of Cumberland, spent several years here as a boy. In 1962 the estate was sold, the old mansion demolished and a new house built on the site, using some of the old bricks, with Dutch style gables and 'Strawberry Gothic' windows.

At first, follow the broad grass track (another old carriage drive) down

Midgham Park

through avenue of oaks, then via a series of gates and stiles along the easily discernible route ahead. Just after crossing drive to main house, notice on left a low brick wall bordering the meadow. This marks the site of an earlier St Matthew's church. The path through the park finally reaches stile at road, to right of white-painted East Lodge. Turn left up lane and at end of field on right, turn right through squeeze-stile and along grass headland. At field corner fork left through gap and follow left-hand boundary of next field to exit at first gap on opposite side. Within a few yards turn left along broad path through middle of this area (Channel Wood) with conifers on right. At end of woodland go through swing-gate and on to driveway past 'Water Oak', towards pretty white Tudor 'Hunts Cottage', Midgham Green.

Turn right up lane, then left at T-junction (signed: 'Bucklebury') for some 70 yards, then cross stile up bank on right and over three small fields to enter Carbins Wood. Follow path ahead across gully and, ignoring turnings left and right, continue straight on, finally passing between two properties on far side of wood. Join gravel drive ahead which leads shortly back to start.

DATE WALKED | | 19

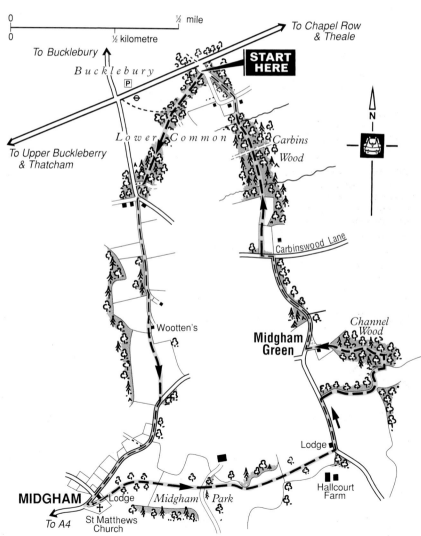

The Slade and Bucklebury Village

A heady mixture of wild common, a hidden hamlet, a popular pub; an almost road-free romp through an ever changing panoply of Berkshire landscape.

Distance: 7 miles
OS Maps: Pathfinder 1187 Newbury;
            1171 Hermitage & Chieveley
Start: Small parking area by
            crossroads (Briff Lane) just
            west of Upper Bucklebury.
            (Grid ref: 537688)

With back to road pass left of notice-board and follow the way-marked path heading more or less straight across the common (crossing road half-way) for nearly a mile, eventually to reach an isolated hamlet, the Slade.

Approaching The Slade

Cross road, pass left of Slade Cottage and follow path between gardens leading to swing-gate. Head straight across grass clearing (ignoring bridleway forking left) to cross lane and shortly enter field at stile. Follow right-hand hedge of first field, then across middle of second, aiming for wide gap in trees on far side. Here a way-mark post

shows the line down past mid-field trees to woodland at bottom of field. Cross footbridge in gully and climb bank ahead, crossing a track (Holly Lane). Go straight on up bank into field and still on same line, climb to top corner of field ahead. Keep to right side of next field, soon to join track and pass to left of Withers Farm.

When level with last farm building, turn left on wide grassy path (Marlston Pightle). Bear left at large tree, cross footbridge and go straight into field to find squeeze-stile left of mid-field oak, with splendid view towards Marlston House (now a school). Maintain direction to bottom of valley, where keep fence on right. At end of garden railings to property on right, turn right and climb track to St Mary's Church.

Cross road and follow right-hand side of first field. At stile take diagonal line across next field and bear left onto track, looking for squeeze-stile shortly on right. Take mid-field line through stiles and over two footbridges (River Pang) to road (Brocks Lane). Turn left for 50 yards, then right, up climbing tree-lined path and along field-edge to join drive (by Gamekeepers Lodge Farm). Follow drive away from house, past front of kennels, to far end of wood. Here turn left through two gates to road, then immediately right, through another swing-gate, into meadows, at far end of which find the welcoming sight of 'Pot Kiln' inn.

Refreshed, we trust, turn right along lane. Where this bends right at top of climb, go straight on through gateway on wide track for 100 yards. Look carefully for path on right which leads through pine trees at first, then down conifer plantation and across open fields to reach stile in hedgerow at top corner of large field with wide views to the horizon. Go down broad mid-field path and then across a paddock to road near New Barn Farm.

Turn left, then shortly right (signed: 'Bucklebury') and after bridge - it's that Pang again - leave road and go straight ahead across field to St Mary's Church.

Pass to right of church tower, continue ahead along village street and after last house on left, turn left up field-edge path. Soon pass to left side of hedge, up steeply climbing path almost concealed in gully. Reaching young plantation on level ground carry on until, on far side of clearing, turn right in front of belt of mature trees ahead. Follow this path until it emerges at field-edge and go half-left towards open valley ahead. Cross footbridge and turn left to follow field-edge with ditch on left until, at start of mature trees ahead, bear right up open field to reach and pass between buildings of Sadgrove Farm.

Turn right along lane and shortly left into byway and then 100 yards beyond old cottage on left turn right up broad track. Just after White Cottage bear right at fork to join lane. From this point go straight ahead for about half a mile, keeping close to properties on left at all times, to return to start.

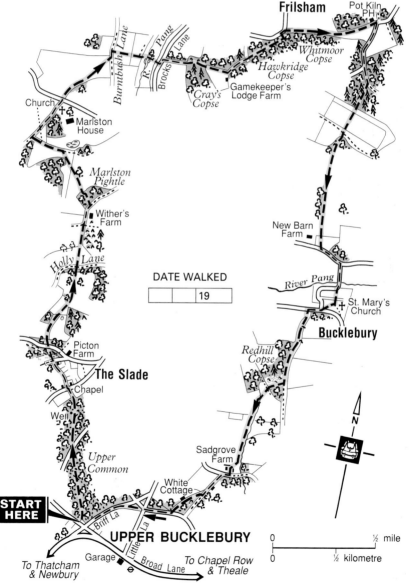

DATE WALKED

| | | 19 |

Box Wood
and Grimsbury Castle

A gently undulating route through the enchanting patchwork of fields and woods centred around Hermitage and the tiny settlement of Oare, the high-spot being the Iron-age hillfort, Grimsbury Castle, in the 375-acre Fence Wood where walkers enjoy full access at all times (Courtesy of The Gerald Palmer Trust).

Distance: 6 miles
OS Map: Pathfinder 1171 Hermitage & Chieveley
Start: Village Hall car park, Hermitage (Grid ref: 506729) or in Marlston Road near church.

Leaving Village Hall (formerly church school, built 1839) turn right and within a few yards right again into Doctor's Lane. At end of wall on left, fork right over stile to follow diagonal line ahead through two fields, with double stile at first boundary. After next stile follow winding path, steadily climbing through bracken-carpeted woodland (Spring Copse) to turn left at path junction (Oare Common).

Go 50 yards beyond cottage on left, then bear right along grassy path with field nearby on right. At lane turn right, shortly to reach Saint Bartholomew's Church, Oare, a delightful little Victorian building (1852) of knapped flint, with an unlocked door! The history of this tiny hamlet goes back to 968 when King Edgar gave 'Orha' to Abingdon Abbey. If electric power ever replaces the internal combustion engine, Oare may regain its former tranquility!

After the church, turn right at Oare Cottage, to reach stile and follow left side of the meadow. Cross stile by pond and school playing-field to road (B4009) at further stile. Turn right, cross over and take

second turning left, Chapel Lane. Just before bridge, by speed restriction sign, turn left down narrow path and over the one-time Didcot/Newbury line (closed 1946), now a play-area and then continue along lane (through Little Hungerford). At sharp right bend go slightly left, shortly to cross field ahead with fence nearby on left and fine stand of trees away to right. Go over stile into narrow path in wooded strip, passing deep pits of former brick works here. Reaching a stile, bear right across corner of field ahead to stile by gateway and follow broad headland track with woodland (Chalkpit Piece) on right. At road turn left for 75 yards before bearing right over stile, to climb through middle of field, aiming just to right of hilltop

Fence Wood pond - in reflective mood

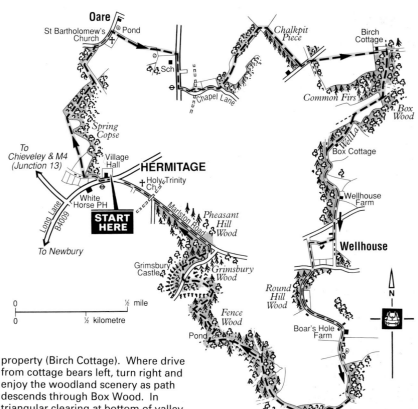

property (Birch Cottage). Where drive from cottage bears left, turn right and enjoy the woodland scenery as path descends through Box Wood. In triangular clearing at bottom of valley turn right over stile and take mid-field path to about half-way point. At this invisible path junction, turn left to stile on field boundary. From this stile keep right, along woodland path studded with mature trees (and fields on left). After property (Box Cottage) track joins from right. Follow this to cross lane and continue on similar track. Beyond pair of cottages bear right across middle of meadow and join drive to right of house. At junction of tracks turn left, shortly to cross road ahead into byway, leading to Boar's Hole Farm.

Pass between farm buildings and continue along track until, where it bends left, turn right through gateway and along field-edge bridleway with mature trees in hedgerow. At end of field pass through metal gate and ahead to junction in front of white cottage, to turn right on bridleway through woodlands (Fence Wood). At far corner of young plantation on left, turn left along grass sward. At end of Christmas trees on left go ahead across staggered

junction and up rising woodland path. At pond turn right. Where stream passes under track, turn left up path between conifers. At next junction turn sharp right soon to reach seat - which has outlived the view!

Turn left by seat to reach top of hill, passing left of turreted house known as Grimsbury Castle, on the site of an Iron-age fort. Go over road into trees, crossing earthwork ditch ahead. Turn right along top of second bank and where this ends continue in same direction with conifers close on left. Reaching road (Marlston Road), turn left downhill back into Hermitage, past the exceedingly plain Holy Trinity Church (1835) with its handsome lych-gate (1947) and so back to start.

DATE WALKED | | | 19 |

Henwick Manor and Red Farm

In this area, historical associations are never far away; this walk is no exception. The same fine views across this dry valley would no doubt have stuck like burrs in Cromwell's mind, as they do in ours today, had he not been directing his forces during the assault on nearby Shaw House and Donnington Castle (Second Battle of Newbury, 1644).

Distance: 6 miles
OS Maps: Pathfinder 1187 Newbury; 1171 Hermitage & Chieveley
Start: Road parking in Lamp Acres, off Long Lane (top of Shaw Hill) B4009, just NE of Newbury (Grid ref: 480685) Easy access on foot from Newbury town centre and Thatcham - see map.

From Lamp Acres turn left along Long Lane. Within a few yards cross road and turn right into narrow footpath alongside Shaw Cemetery. At end of path cross one-time route of Didcot to Newbury railway and turn left along gravel track. At end of track enter field ahead and turn right, uphill, aiming for gap in trees, there to continue on same line over rough grazing area, to cross stile in top corner. Admire the views while recharging your lungs! After short length of fenced path turn left along road (Stoney Lane). Watch out for Sherpas along here!

After last of properties on right, turn right along fenced path, soon with trees on right (Stoney Copse). At stile enter field ahead and bear half-right to pass left-hand end of tree-belt (Sett Copse) to reach junction of ways. Here bear left along farm track, enjoying the wide views across the Kennet Valley, towards Newbury racecourse and beyond. Follow this track down through farmyard at Henwick Manor.

Just beyond farm buildings leave concrete drive to go straight along track ahead until, just past Manor Cottage, leave track over stile on right. Maintain same direction across field to cross pair of stiles, then narrow meadow, to plank-bridge and squeeze-stile ahead. (Footpath from Thatcham joins our route here - see map.)

After squeeze-stile follow ditch on left through two fields, then turn left over footbridge and up midfield, aiming for second stile, to left of barn. On same line continue across small field to swing-gate on right of modern house, Northcroft Farm. Beyond house take shingle path to stile and turn right along road through Ashmore Green. Immediately before Garage turn left

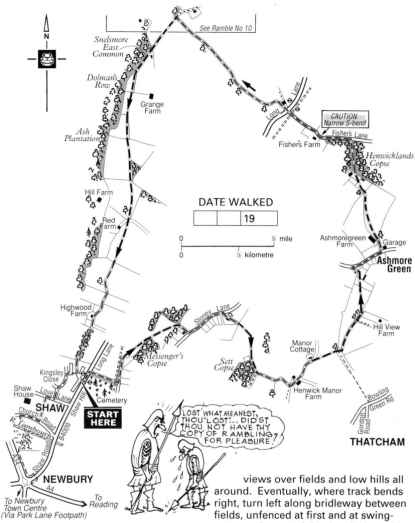

DATE WALKED

		19

along scruffy little path and over two stiles. Cross concrete track, ignore field-gate on right and continue ahead with farm to left, shortly to enter field over stile/plank bridge. Here take diagonal line (angle shown by signpost arm) to stile near furthest corner. Follow bushes half-way along left side of first paddock then bear right, aiming to pass just to right of cream-painted house, and then along drive to turn left along road (Fishers Lane).

Carefully navigate S-bend in lane past Fishers Farm and at cross-roads (Long Lane) go straight ahead along farm track for nearly ¾ mile, with wide-ranging

views over fields and low hills all around. Eventually, where track bends right, turn left along bridleway between fields, unfenced at first and at swing-gate continue straight ahead, alongside copse on right (bordering Snelsmore East Common).

Directions now seem superfluous, as the slowly descending bridleway links the fields, like charms on a bracelet, leaving the walker free to enjoy the delightful pastoral scenery - look out for the many deer in this area.

After several fields, cross tarmac drive (to Red Farm) and carry on in same direction, with appropriately coloured barn nearby on right. A bridle-gate ahead into an enclosed path leads on to a drive past house on right (Highwood Farm), then shrinks again between hedges, leading shortly back to start.

Curridge Village and Chalky Lane

A short, easy going stroll through the well-wooded countryside still to be found within a stone's throw of the M4 motorway, around the small village of Curridge. From such an unlikely starting point it is possible to see deer in a bluebell wood within fifteen minutes.

Distance: 3 miles; see map for link to 6 mile Ramble 9

OS Map: Pathfinder 1171 Hermitage & Chieveley

Start: Car park at Granada Chieveley Services on A34, SE side of M4 (J.13) 2 hours free parking (Grid ref: 481727)

Facing restaurant entrance, turn left along pavement and with due care cross filling-station exit lanes to reach grass bank of traffic island ahead. Turn left along bank and over slip-road (access to M4), again to turn left along hedge-topped grass bank. When level with end of lorry park, turn right into field opening, then immediately right again, past green metal gate and head diagonally to middle of field, just to left of solitary tree. At this seemingly improbable point, the right of way changes direction and bears left to another lone tree close to the woodland ahead - Lanolee Copse.

Leave field by footbridge over ditch, turn left and at end of copse turn right along woodland path. Bear left at fork and as path climbs (between Lanolee and Smithy Copses) ignore paths on either side to reach stile at field edge. Cross two fields ahead and finally, after stile and squeeze-way, turn right at 'The Georgian House' into pot-holed track, known as Chapel Lane. (For access for nearby pub, 'The Bunk' - see map.)

Where lane bends sharp left, go straight ahead along gravel path, shortly to reach Curridge County Primary School. An unusual design: built originally in 1856 combining church and school, hence apse-shaped end. Just a school since 1966. Continue on tarmac drive and after crossing road ahead, turn right for a few yards before turning left into broad unmade road. The house on the corner, the Old Parsonage, was once the home

of H M Bateman, the famous cartoonist. Land behind the house is known as Curridge Green, once the centre of village events, sadly now enclosed.

In front of stables ahead, turn right along tree-lined track, passing two properties before reaching junction. Ignore tracks to right and left and go straight on along bridleway between fields, unfenced at first, to find swing-gate at corner of wood. (See map for link to Ramble 9.)

After swing-gate, immediately turn right into wood (part of Snelsmore East Common). Keep to right in copse and soon cross stile into fenced path, passing property on right. On reaching lane (Curridge Road) by entrance to 'Foxford', turn left. We shall be turning right at end of first field on right but to avoid road walking, after Vine Cottage use edge of common on left, before crossing Curridge Road to enter byway at metal gate. This may be called Chalky Lane but the chalk has not helped the drainage, so use edge of wood if muddy. Follow this track for more than a mile through Grigg's Copse, then Breach Copse, eventually to emerge facing the clamorous A34. Here bear right along field end and then, where possible using grass verge alongside slip-road, return to car park at start.

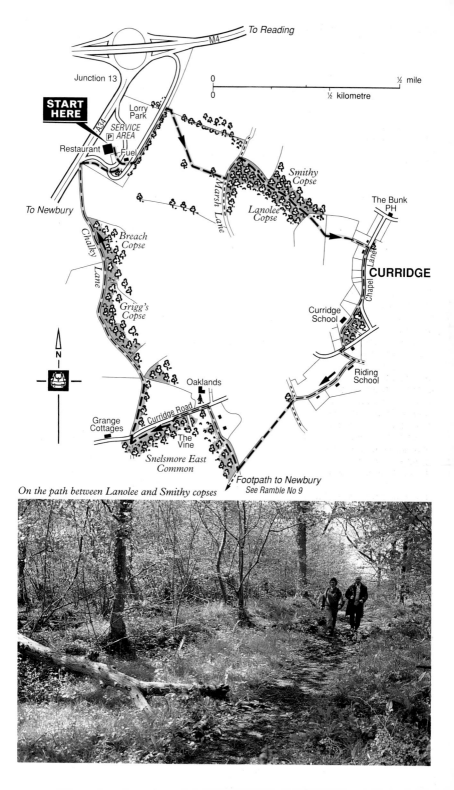

To Reading

M4

Junction 13

START HERE

A34

Lorry Park

SERVICE AREA

P

Restaurant

Fuel

To Newbury

Marsh Lane

Smithy Copse

Lanolee Copse

The Bunk PH

Chalky Lane

Breach Copse

Grigg's Copse

N

CURRIDGE

Chapel Lane

Curridge School

Oaklands

Curridge Road

Riding School

Grange Cottages

The Vine

Snelsmore East Common

Footpath to Newbury
See Ramble No 9

0 ————— ½ mile
0 ————— ½ kilometre

On the path between Lanolee and Smithy copses

Winterbourne Village and Boxford Common

'Lovely to look at, delightful to know' may be cue for a song, but it is also cue for this walk, which has just about everything; old villages, splendid houses, beautiful scenery, a wild common, all linked together by some fine paths.

Distance: 6 miles
OS Maps: Pathfinder 1187 Newbury; 1171 Hermitage
Start: Snelsmore Common Country Park (Grid ref: 464710)

With back to road enter Country Park and fork right along tarmac drive past parking areas. 30 yards after metal (car) barrier bear right onto gravel track. Where track forks at fire beater stand bear right, then left, onto a clear track across common, soon to cross under power-lines and enter woodland (Withy Copse) down steep stony path. Bear right along edge of woods to reach and turn left along narrow lane. When level with Georgian property (Winterbourne Holt, beautifully positioned for views fore and aft), turn right off lane, keeping close to wood but dropping down to find swing-gate in field corner. Follow wood in next field to another swing-gate, then cross a stile. Take mid-field path ahead (some 25 yards to right of power-lines) and go through three fields with stiles between. Reaching final field-side to right of houses, cross Winterbourne Stream, giving its name to this delightful village (and pub) that you have now reached. Opposite the pub do notice an old enamel AA sign.

Turn left along village street until just beyond thatched cottage, opposite the diminutive 'Pedlars', turn right through wooden gates and up past garage to reach field. A few paces into field turn right up steps in bank, then climb field-edge path which soon continues 'inside' hedgerow, to emerge as climbing track between open fields and finally enters churchyard (St James the Less).

Winterbourne claims a slight brush with history; it is said that Oliver Cromwell attended the tiny church here on the eve of the Second Battle of Newbury. The next day, 27 October 1644, the *Parliamentary army passed through here from their overnight camp at nearby North Heath, en route to Boxford and Wickham Heath.*

Pass church porch, leave by gate facing Manor House and turn right along track between farm buildings and then ahead between open fields, to pass to right of buildings ahead (Lower Farm). Turn left past back of farm, to continue on grassy track, then go ahead across corner of wood (Wyfield Copse) and follow fence of field on right to enter meadow at swing-gate. The path line follows right-hand field boundary as it circles to left (avoid gateway) and continue through two adjoining fields, with woodland strip on right and fine views ahead over Kennet Valley to Watership Down on horizon. At bottom of third field cross stile and turn right along road until, just before top of rise, cross stile in fence on left into woods.

After 40 yards bear left along narrow way-marked path soon joining a wider one. Look carefully for right-hand fork (at way-mark post) and follow this narrower path to cross stile into field. Stay on same line over next stile and then through middle of large field (Boxford Common) towards far right-hand corner. Cross stile into woodland and bear right, shortly down slope. At field-side continue ahead but to right of hedgerow to reach stile next to gate. Now follow this track straight ahead for about half-a-mile. Panoramic vision would be useful here to take in the contours, left towards the Winterbourne Valley, right towards the Lambourn Valley,

At bottom of slope, just after lane joins from right, turn left into first field entrance and go diagonally across to far corner, then over three stiles close together and a fourth at road. Turn left, then right, along Bagnor village street (see map for features) and just beyond large white cottage turn left up through field to copse. Cross stile and turn left on a long, uncomfortably 'stumpy' path between trees, with golf course above on right. Path joins drive and passes left of Honey Bottom Cottage. Continue on

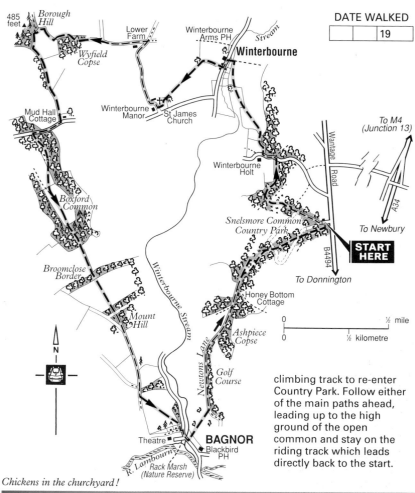

DATE WALKED

| | | 19 |

485 feet

Borough Hill

Lower Farm

Winterbourne Arms PH

Stream

Winterbourne

Wyfield Copse

Mud Hall Cottage

Winterbourne Manor · St James Church

To M4 (Junction 13)

A34

Wantage Road

Boxford Common

Winterbourne Holt

To Newbury

Snelsmore Common Country Park

START HERE

Broomclose Border

B4494

To Donnington

Mount Hill

Honey Bottom Cottage

Winterbourne Stream

Newtons Lane

Ashpiece Copse

0 ———————————— ½ mile
0 ———————————— ½ kilometre

Golf Course

climbing track to re-enter Country Park. Follow either of the main paths ahead, leading up to the high ground of the open common and stay on the riding track which leads directly back to the start.

N

Theatre ■ **BAGNOR**
Blackbird PH

R. Lambourn
Rack Marsh (Nature Reserve)

Chickens in the churchyard!

Speen Moor and Hamstead Park

Walking through the tranquil scenery east of Enborne, it is hard to imagine that 6,000 men met their deaths here one autumn day in 1643, at the First Battle of Newbury. Ironically, the recent planning battle over building a by-pass will have a much greater effect on the landscape.

Distance: 8 miles
OS Maps: Pathfinder 1187 Newbury
Start: Newbury BR Station (Grid ref: 471668) See map for alternative starting points such as Northcroft Recreation Centre (Grid ref: 465673)

With back to station (north side) head diagonally across car park (signed Town Centre), up concrete steps, past Council Offices on left, over minor road and ahead through Inch's Yard. Cross 'zebra' to join left-hand footway (Bartholomew St) with clock-tower ahead. At traffic lights go ahead over bridge and within a few paces turn left down narrow passage signed 'Newbury Lock'. Follow towpath of Kennet & Avon Canal past lock. By Dolton Mews cross canal by swing-bridge, to continue in same direction on other bank, along West Mills.

At footbridge (Monkey Bridge) re-cross canal and follow path (part of Lambourn Valley Way) to right of Northcroft Recreation Centre (fancy a swim?). Turn left along avenue of lime trees, then left again along gravel track (Moor Lane) between properties. Notice Thames Water's 'Speen Depot' on left and soon pass under arch of one-time Lambourn branch line, 'axed' by Dr Beeching in 1960. Path goes left of property, through swing-gate, bearing right between hedges, the start of Speen Moor.

Continue along raised path until, some 40 yards past line of poplars, turn right over stile to follow hedged track climbing to gate at Bath Road (A4). With care cross over, turning left along footway, soon to pass entrance to

Benham Valance Park. (Don't despair, the best is yet to come!) 200 yards beyond weathered milestone (bearing the score 'Newbury 2 - Hungerford 7') re-cross road and, with sigh of relief, leave traffic behind as you pass through wooden gate into shrubery of the Park. Shortly fork left and follow slightly sunken path to emerge at top of open park-land. Descend through this 18th century landscape on wide grassy path, murmuring 'thank you' to Capability Brown. Cross stile at bottom corner and follow gravel drive, becoming tarmac, to reach road at lodge gates. Continue ahead past the 'Water Rat' and at crossroads turn left. After level-crossing, pass Marsh Benham House to reach Hamstead Lock. At this point the canal path on left leads back to Newbury (3 miles) saving about ½ mile, and a climb, on our route - see map.

To continue, cross River Kennet and within a few yards go over stile on left into the 700-acre Hamstead Park, for 300 years seat of the

Earls of Craven. Follow drive as it winds uphill, soon with view over lake. Just beyond top of climb, path leaves drive and runs alongside tall hedge. Continue ahead, soon to join and bear left along tree-lined drive. Notice behind you the 18th century mansion. View on right here is towards Walbury Hill (974 ft), highest point in Berkshire.

Follow drive round to the road and go straight across to visit Enborne's Norman church of St Michael. Returning to road, turn right and shortly right again into Church Lane. At beginning of slope turn left into path by Old Lane Cottage. Some of the paths ahead will be diverted by construction of Newbury by-pass but in the meantime pass through squeeze-stile and ahead to footbridge at end of first field. In next field maintain same direction, diagonally, to go through woodland strip on far side. Path ahead crosses corner of field then along hedgerow on left. At path crossing, turn left at stile and over next field to find steps up embankment. Now turn left for

Follow the drive through Hamstead Park

15 yards and descend on other side, aiming for left-hand end of Skinners Green Farm ahead. Turn left along path in front of buildings and left again at road. Where road turns left, go ahead along hedged track, then field edge, to cross gully by plank bridge. Now follow right-hand side of fields to emerge at edge of town, keeping straight on (along Fifth Rd.), eventually to reach T-junction.

Cross over, turn left for 40 paces, then turn right on tarmac path to left of playing-field. Exit through gates, go ahead along foot-way past 'Red House' and delightful old buildings in Argyle Road. Cross ahead at road junction and turn right into Station Road to return to start.

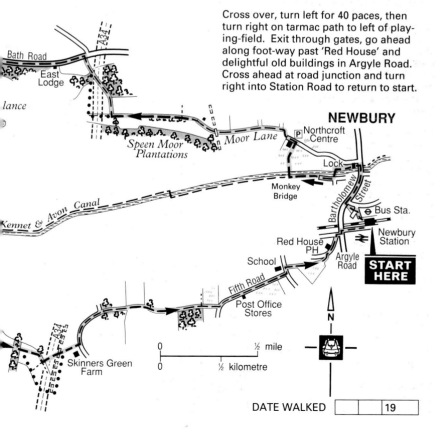

DATE WALKED   19

Newtown Common and Horris Hill

So near (to Newbury), yet so far from the madding crowd. This figure of eight walk loops the loop around the modest slopes of Horris Hill and this age-old Common. Once upon a time Newtown Common could boast its own school, shop, gun-smith, besom maker. Come with us and we'll show you where they were...

Distance: 4 miles
OS Map: Pathfinder 1187 Newbury
Start: 2 miles S of Newbury (road to Burghclere). Parking space on edge of Newtown Common, top of Jonathan Hill. (Grid ref: 477633)

With back to road junction, take wide main track ahead, shortly forking right on footpath past metal barrier, soon to follow edge of Common with fields on left. Keep to main track (a 'permitted bridleway') as it bears right, on a line slightly to left of overhead cables. Reaching tarmac drive turn right, leading to road junction. Cross over and continue ahead along gravel track (Sheepwash Lane) which dips down to stream - clearly for small sheep - to reach and cross noisome A34 trunk road.

On other side of road be sure not to turn left but go straight ahead on narrow path which dips down under power-lines. Then take the left-hand fork, way-marked (white arrows) through trees, which descends to lane junction.

Follow lane past white house, 'The Bothy' and climb track to pass between the playing-fields and scattered buildings of Horris Hill School. (Many a whack on willow here on a summer's day.) Continue on track past 'Hill End' descending to bear left along metalled road. Where road bends right, turn left at metal gate and follow right-hand hedgerow, to finally leave fields at further metal gate, turning left down broad tree-lined track. After Wheatlands Farm and other properties, where lane (Deadmoor Lane) bends right, turn sharp left through white gate - 'Heatherwold' - and within a few yards cross stile and follow right-hand side of paddocks. Path ahead dips in and out of thicket, via stiles either end, before turning through green metal gate on right and along left side of field to leave by swing-gate, thus completing the loop back to 'The Bothy'.

Turn right down lane, then left at first corner and climb steadily, keeping to main track. Soon after old cottage, 'Byways', notice on left NT plaque for 'Barn Plot'. This ¼ acre was given by a Mr T Shaw in 1906 - one of the Trust's smallest properties. At post-box ahead carefully cross busy road and maintain same direction on path through woodland leading to tile-hung cottage.

This cottage was built in 1827 for the school-mistress with its adjoining school-room, now garages. The next property, 'Coxs' was once the village shop (note typical window) and just beyond this was a gun-smith's.

Follow hedge fronting 'Coxs' and find little sunken path leading to stile onto

parkland. Now head for stile shortly on left into pine copse. Path bears left, crosses footbridge, then climbs bank between holly bushes before dipping down to left and along a level, almost terraced path, with pleasant views on left. Ignore turning on right before crossing road ahead - by 'Woodcote' - and up track opposite. Shortly turn right (with Village Hall to left), then left and right to pass pair of thatched cottages and along short track back to start.

DATE WALKED [| | 19]

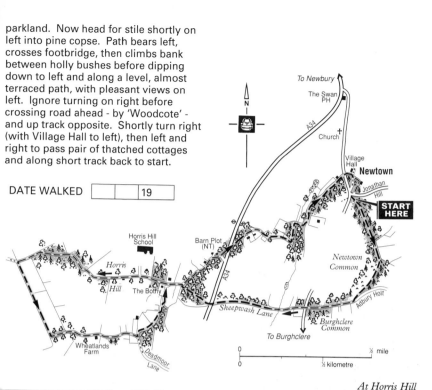

At Horris Hill

Publications

Each illustrated booklet contains twenty or more short circular walks.

Rambling for Pleasure in East Berkshire (1st series) £1.20
Rambling for Pleasure in East Berkshire (2nd series)..£1.20
Rambling for Pleasure Around Reading (1st series)..£1.75
Rambling for Pleasure Around Reading (2nd series) £1.75
Rambling for Pleasure Along the Thames (full colour) £2.50
The Three Castles Path (Long Distance Path) £2.50
Footpath Map
Windsor and The Great Park (Two colour A3 size)..50p

All these publications, including this booklet, are avalable from local bookshops and stationers or by post 40p extra (cheques payable to East Berk RA Group) from:
Pat Hayers, 16 Lanterns Walk, Farthingales, Maidenhead, Berkshire SL6 1TG

Burghclere Brook and Sydmonton Common

A walk with a difference; a short bus ride from Newbury enables walkers to use some delightful paths through woods and meadows west of Headley, including half a mile of rights of way which have been reopened as a direct result of this publication. Motorists start at 2.

Distance: 1. 2½ miles 2. 3 miles
OS Map: Pathfinder 1187 Newbury
Start: 1. Bus route 32 from Newbury (hourly Mon-Sat), alight 'Adbury turn'
2. Park at southern end of lay-by (old road by Knightsbridge Barn), off A339, 4 miles SE of Newbury (Grid ref: 507633)

Start 1. From bus-stop, go down lane signed 'Sandford Memorial Chapel' and over River Enborne (Berks/Hants boundary) at Aldern Bridge. At end of field on left, turn left through second rusty gate and take diagonal field-path to gap in far hedgerow just left of large

tree. To be correct, this path turns left before the hedge but, instead, go through the gap and turn left along headland with trees and ditch on left. At bottom field corner turn right for some 35 yards, then turn left down bank. Cross grass strip and over the babbling Burghclere Brook, then up way-marked woodland path (Sydmonton Common). Reaching wide crossing track turn right for 125 paces (to be safe, count them) then turn left up bank into recently reopened footpath. Skip next paragraph.

Start 2. With back to Knightsbridge Barn, at north end of lay-by, carefully cross main road, turn right past bus-stop and cross plank-bridge over ditch. Take diagonal cross-field line to stile in right-hand corner and then follow bank of River Enborne. From stile into next field, head mid-field at first, then follow hedge on left. Just beyond end of Works, turn left across drive, to stile in top corner of field. Turn left and cross road - this is the hamlet of Bishops Green. After property on right, by large yew tree, turn right along track, soon narrowing to grass path between paddocks. Footbridge leads into mixed woodland, known as Sydmonton

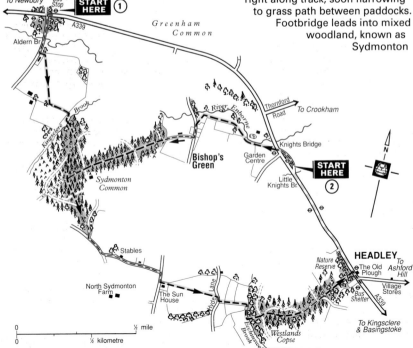

Common. Follow path ahead, rutted at first, straight through woodland. Disregard other tracks until finally, about 25 yards BEFORE end of tall pines on RIGHT, turn left on recently reopened narrow crossing footpath.

Now follow this delightful woodland path until finally leaving canopy of trees, continue ahead on broad gravel track which joins from right. At junction with drive, bear right to end of woods and go straight on along lane. At junction with private road to North Sydmonton Farm (note distant views of North Hampshire Downs) bear left, passing stables. At next road junction turn right, then shortly left, over two stiles to left of house, formerly the 'Rising Sun' inn. Locals recall running, tankards in hand, round the triangle formed by the 'Sun', the 'Plough' and the 'Harrow'. Today, only the 'Harrow' survives.

From field corner take mid-field line down to stile, turning right along road (Hyde Lane). Where lane bends right, turn left over stile and go straight down through two meadows, to turn right through field gate and along valley bottom for 100 yards. Here, turn left over footbridge straddling Ecchinswell

Brook and climb narrow path between the trees of Westlands Copse. Joining track ahead, continue up it for 40 yards then stay on same line into conifers on way-marked path. Near top of slope emerge from trees to follow wide track ahead and where this bears right be sure not to miss the narrow path STRAIGHT ON at this point. This re-established path through the trees soon meets a kissing-gate and goes straight on across a lightly-wooded area.

This is the Headley Gravel Pit reserve managed by the Hampshire Wildlife Trust. The principal attraction here is the huge population of Green-winged Orchids - thousands carpet the ground each May. An unusual number of melanistic snakes means this is also home to the Black Adder!

At main road (A339), opposite 'Robins Grove', carefully cross over and turn right, to pass the previously mentioned one-time 'Plough' inn. (The 'Harrow' is but a few minutes walk ahead.) Opposite the end of Ashford Hill Road is the return bus-stop. At the next stop, Knights Bridge, walkers will be re-united with their cars.

DATE WALKED [   ] [19]

The Burghclere Triangle

This is a walk on the 'titled' side; through a wide variety of scenery over two large estates, owned by the 7th Earl of Carnarvon (Racing Manager to HM The Queen), and the first Sir Andrew Lloyd Webber (prince of song writers). Look out for hidden gems, such as Earlstone Manor.

Distance: 7 miles (see map for shorter alternative)

OS Maps: Pathfinder 1187 Newbury; 1203 Kingsclere

Start: Park alongside church, in Church Lane, Burghclere - 4 miles S of Newbury (Grid ref: 470611)

FIRST LEG (2 miles)

With back to church, cross Church Lane and turn right along Harts Lane, soon passing village shop (chance to stock up!) At junction by 'The Queen' go ahead and at bottom of dip turn right along tree-lined track (edge of Earlstone Common). Shortly, at road crossing, go straight on along drive, bearing right at Bearstone House, soon to reach stile by metal gate. Follow track ahead, bearing left between farm buildings and the delightful old Palmer's Hill House.

The path ahead leisurely weaves its way to reach prominent crossing track. Stay on same line on rising grass-lined mid-field path until, at top of slope, a panorama unfolds of North Hampshire downland, rising to highest point on right - Beacon Hill. Continue on over open field to enter woodland and cross concrete bridge to road. Turn left for 30 yards, then right, up bank. The line ahead, through middle of 3 fields, is slightly left from this point, to stile at first field boundary. In second field, aim for large gap in far corner; in third field head for centre of distant tall trees.

SECOND LEG (3 miles)

About 25 yards before marker-post on far side of this third field, turn very sharp right (precise line of right of way), passing to left of solitary tree, towards definite kink in field boundary. Here path enters trees (Waterleas Copse) and crosses Burghclere Brook. Soon bear right along gravel farm track and at end of field turn left along headland. At end of conifer block turn right along path to far side of woodland strip, then left along field-edge leading to road. Cross lane to right, signed 'Woodside Dairy Unit' and follow concrete drive between buildings, down slope, then half-left across field to gateway. Now head mid-field to cross stile and along edge of next field with copse on left (Lower Berry Wood). At end of copse, continue across field on same line, passing some 30 yards to left of distant tall tree. Maintain this distance from field side until, at very lowest point, bear right to cross stream (Earlstone Brook) at culvert in trees. Pass to right of pond and head up slope to meet drive at Earlstone Manor.

Turn left down drive through gateway and at top of rise just ahead, turn right down bank and follow hedged bridleway for some distance to reach road. Bear right along higher lane (signed 'Old Burghclere') and, where lane joins from right, turn right, down bank, to cross stile at start of long, thin field, with stream on right. In next field, keep hedge-topped bank on right. Cross culvert in further field, turn right, round two sides to enter woodland at swing-gate.

After small poplar plantation, path follows bank, becoming grassy track along bottom of wooded valley (Ware Copse). About ten paces before path meets prominent track (in fact, line of dismantled railway), turn left up bank and along field-edge ahead. (Across to left is Ladle Hill, visited on Ramble 16.) At road, turn right over bridge. At crossroads, a few yards to left stands one-time Burghclere Station; ahead you may visit Old Burghclere Church just beyond Manor House, with open views and footpath to Beacon Hill.

THIRD LEG (2 miles)

Returning from church, turn left along lane past Manor Farm (part of 6,500 acre

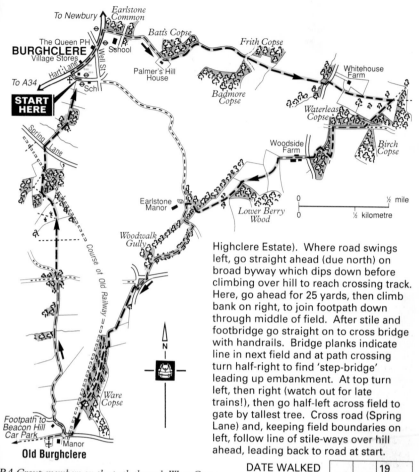

To Newbury

Earlstone Common

Batt's Copse

Frith Copse

The Queen PH

BURGHCLERE
Village Stores

School

Palmer's Hill House

To A34

Well St

Hart Lane

START HERE

Sch

Badmore Copse

Whitehouse Farm

Waterleas Copse

Birch Copse

Woodside Farm

Spring Lane

Course of Old Railway

Earlstone Manor

Lower Berry Wood

Woodwalk Gully

0   ½ mile
0   ½ kilometre

N

Ware Copse

Footpath to Beacon Hill Car Park

Manor

Old Burghclere

Highclere Estate). Where road swings left, go straight ahead (due north) on broad byway which dips down before climbing over hill to reach crossing track. Here, go ahead for 25 yards, then climb bank on right, to join footpath down through middle of field. After stile and footbridge go straight on to cross bridge with handrails. Bridge planks indicate line in next field and at path crossing turn half-right to find 'step-bridge' leading up embankment. At top turn left, then right (watch out for late trains!), then go half-left across field to gate by tallest tree. Cross road (Spring Lane) and, keeping field boundaries on left, follow line of stile-ways over hill ahead, leading back to road at start.

RA Group members on the path through Ware Copse

DATE WALKED | | 19

Ladle Hill and Sydmonton

If you feel 'activity challenged', this could be the answer. From the well-heeled acres of the Sydmonton Estate, deep in quiet countryside, climb some 360 feet to the historic heights of an Iron-age fort. Then switch the scenery to 'fast forward' as you descend, leaving memorable images on the retina.

Distance: 4 miles
OS Map: Pathfinder 1203 Kingsclere
Start: Verge parking at lane junction, facing Lodge of Sydmonton Court, 1¼ miles E of A34, 3½ miles W of Kingsclere. (Grid ref: 478580)

Facing Lodge and drive to Sydmonton Court turn left along lane (signed 'Burghclere 2'). At end of Wergs Farm buildings - do notice thatched barn at one point - turn right along open gravel drive, passing pair of houses on left. On reaching crossing drive, turn sharp right and over stile by wooden gates.

Follow drive to reach two stately cedar trees framing the approach to Sydmonton Court, an 'ancient commodious mansion', presently the country home of Sir Andrew Lloyd Webber. The right of way continues straight ahead, gravel drive becoming wide grass strip.

According to Pevsner, 'The house seems to present a complicated architectural history. It ought to be unravelled.' Notice on left an old 'VR' wall letter box - 'Cleared at 4.30 pm - Sundays 11.5 am' states Kelly's Directory of 1907. Also catch a glimpse here through trees of the now redundant St Mary's Norman church, rebuilt 1853, no longer accessible to the public.

Reaching road turn left and shortly, after farmhouse, turn right over stile into wide, hedged track. As track climbs steadily there are views to left towards Watership Down. Where track divides, bear left up gully and keep left again after stile by gate (into Barton Copse). As path continues to climb, the sheep-studded turf of the Downs comes into view over bank on left, revealing a natural masterpiece of gentle curves,

sweeping down the chalk scarp to an isolated cottage far below. Is it any wonder that while living there, at Shepherds Cottage, author Richard Adams was inspired to write the instant best-seller 'Watership Down'?

Tear yourself away from the view and continue to top of track and turn right over stile, to join the North Hampshire Ridgeway path (also known today as the Wayfarers Walk), along the crest of the Downs. Ancient barrows and hill-forts along this prehistoric trackway are evidence of its use for over 4,000 years.

After a bridle-gate follow top of Downs curving left with fine views on right back over Sydmonton. Immediately, after another swing-gate turn left, then shortly right, with fields both sides, passing tumuli nearby on left. Path climbs gently to the breezy summit of Ladle Hill, an unfinished Iron-age hill-fort, fenced off on right, giving a clear view across the A34 below, to Beacon Hill, at 872 ft the highest spot on these Downs.

About 100 yards BEFORE two small trees ahead on right (marking an earthwork), turn sharp right, back across field. The stony path becomes a well-beaten track as it descends the shoulder of Ladle Hill through delightful scenery for a mile, eventually reaching road at starting point.

Passing Sydmonton Court ~ focal point of the walk

DATE WALKED [   ] [19]

Winter views over Nuthanger Down

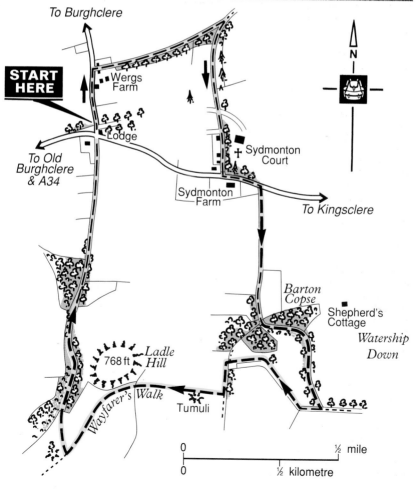

To Burghclere

START HERE

Wergs Farm

Lodge

To Old Burghclere & A34

Sydmonton Court

Sydmonton Farm

To Kingsclere

N

Barton Copse

Shepherd's Cottage

Watership Down

768 ft
Ladle Hill

Wayfarer's Walk

Tumuli

0   ½ mile

0   ½ kilometre

Ecchinswell and Nuthanger Farm

The place-names along this delightful walk should start bells ringing for followers of Hazel, Fiver, Bigwig and the other characters in Richard Adams' furry-story of 'Watership Down'. In this inspiring countryside even the birds may be whistling the latest melodies from the prolific Sir Andrew Lloyd Webber, 'squire' of these parts.

Distance: 4 or 5 miles
OS Maps: Pathfinder 1203 Kingsclere; 1187 Newbury
Start: Ecchinswell village hall car park, 6 miles SE of Newbury. (Grid ref: 500596)

From car park turn right along road and just past pretty Victorian school-house turn left (Mill Lane). Where tarmac ends beyond mill, continue on grass path to right of 'Elderfield', leading to stile into fenced path. At next stile turn right along broad grass headland and in following field aim diagonally towards tallest tree to reach road.

Turn left along road and then right, thirty yards beyond entrance to Clere House. This broad grass path becomes a raised tree-lined ridge, with the whimsically-named Nothing Hill away on left. Path stops, facing trees ahead (Nuthanger Copse) and until the old track through the copse is reopened we must trace its line along edge of field to left. At end of copse path bears right, soon with trees close on right again. Wonderful views all around, especially to left, of

Watership Down and the Beech Hanger featured in Richard Adams' story. On reaching gravel track turn right and in front of farm entrance (Nuthanger Farm) ahead, turn left past white metal gate. Follow drive until, with house entrance straight ahead, turn right through another white gate.

Away to left distant glimpse possible of Highclere Castle, seat of the Earls of Carnarvon. While not a castle, it is the largest mansion in Hampshire, designed in 1840 by Sir Charles Barry, architect of the Houses of Parliament.

Tarmac drive descends, becoming narrow path through green metal gates on right of stables. Follow track, then headland, to reach stile by gate leading to a somewhat quaint holding by roadside. Within a few paces along road turn sharp left into drive (Sydmonton Court Estate). At buildings on right (Watership Farm) continue straight on along drive and at T-junction turn right to climb past group of estate houses (Laundry Cottages) eventually to emerge at road.

Here go ahead along quiet lane and shortly after farm cottage/buildings on left (Cowhouse Farm) look for double gates on right which mark the turning for shorter route. For this, follow gravel track until it turns left, at which point go straight on along grass headland to enter village playing-field. Keep to left of field to return to start.

The broad grass path becomes....

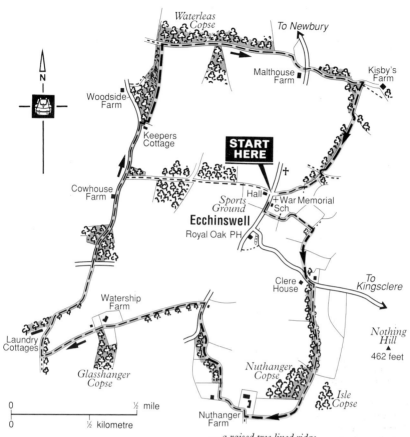

Waterleas Copse

To Newbury

Malthouse Farm

Kisby's Farm

N

Woodside Farm

Keepers Cottage

START HERE

Cowhouse Farm

Hall

+ War Memorial

Sports Ground

Sch

Ecchinswell

Royal Oak PH

Clere House

To Kingsclere

Watership Farm

Nothing Hill ▲ 462 feet

Laundry Cottages

Glasshanger Copse

Nuthanger Copse

Isle Copse

Nuthanger Farm

0		½ mile
0		½ kilometre

....a raised tree lined ridge

For the longer walk, continue along lane as far as Keepers Cottage. Here bear right across gravel drive, over stile into wood and along cottage boundary. Enter field and turn left along field-edge with woodland on left. At far end of field turn right on broad farm track, with woodland (Waterleas Copse) on left. Follow track to reach buildings of Malthouse Farm. In front of large store, bear left to road. Cross road and go ahead, passing 'semi-dethatched' cottage. At bend in drive, with pink-washed walls of Kisby's Farm in view ahead, turn sharp right into broad, hedged track. At end of wide section cross stile ahead and follow right-hand side of long meadow, to leave near far end over stile by gate on right. At path junction turn left for 40 yards. Cross stream (Ecchinswell Brook), turn right over sleeper bridge and then over stile ahead into field. Look for stile on right to recross stream and after two small bridges follow path beside bank to emerge by War Memorial and the start.

DATE WALKED [ ] [19]

Watership Down and Cottington's Hill

Here is a walk to satisfy that 'let's get away from it all' feeling. Climb to the heady delights of the North Hampshire Downs which inspired Richard Adams' classic fable 'Watership Down', already a familiar landmark on the literary map. And don't miss the site of King John's hideaway on the way back.

Distance: 6½ or 5¾ miles
OS Map: Pathfinder 1203 Kingsclere
Start: Free public car park off Swan Street, Kingsclere (Grid ref: 525586)

From entrance to car park go straight ahead down Anchor Road and across Swan Street into St Mary's churchyard. This sturdy Norman-style, flint-faced church was extensively rebuilt in 1848. Note the bed-bug weather-vane said to recall King John's uncomfortable night at a local hostelry.

Follow tarmac path to left of church and between wooden posts out of church-yard. Facing panel fence, turn right into narrow enclosed path over two footbridges, leading to stile at road. Here turn left (Foxs Lane) and go past road junction to where country starts.

Continue along road using verge where possible. About 100 yards after passing under power-lines, turn left by single white metal gate and go straight ahead alongside grass gallop. At end of first field on left, bear left on right of way between open fields. At T-junction turn right up farm track to a point level with top of second field on right. Here turn left up slope for 50 yards through cluster of trees to cross stile onto rough hillside. Take a few deep breaths, then climb path going half-right, finally to reach an iso-lated stile alongside the gallops on Cannon Heath Down.

Now stride along the splendid downland to reach Watership Down, enjoying the scenery below and the skylarks above. Cross the next stile and immediately bear half-left for 50 yards to edge of main gallops. Continue on same line, aiming for tallest trees (Cannon Avenue), to go through swing-gate and turn sharp left along chalk track. Devotees of

Richard Adams' story may turn right for some yards to view 'Bigwig's tree', a huge beech, and to recall the line: "from under the Beech Hanger...you can see the whole World." Nice spot for a picnic.

To continue, follow this ancient chalk trackway - the North Hampshire Ridgeway - with gallops on both sides, to reach B3051 at White Hill. Carefully cross busy road and within 30 paces turn sharp right along narrow path between trees, shortly to turn left over stile and climb right-hand headland through two fields with stile between (Stubbington Down). At top of first field look for shorter circuit - see map - but beware of steep slope, especially when wet. At top of second field our main circuit turns left but the grassy track ahead, over the ugly metal stile, leads within minutes to the site of an Iron-age fort.

History records that 800 years ago King John regularly visited a small castle and hunting lodge he had built here, called Freemantle. Now, only dried-up remains of medieval fish-ponds mark the spot, in the field beyond the BBC TV mast which today teeters on this 751 ft summit.

Returning to our circular route, follow top boundary of field and where this turns right, along edge of wood, keep straight on across middle of field, steeply down to cross stile on far side. Turn right along path confined between thorn thicket and wire fence. At end of thicket cross stile (off line) and follow broad ride through conifers (Coronation Plantation).

Plantation gives way to downland grass. Follow ribbon of pine trees on right, then fence, finally to cross stile in far corner of field. Here turn left down farm track which dwindles to a bridleway across a wide tract of farmland. On reaching far side, at once bear left into narrow tree-lined path (Hollowshot La.). Eventually, just before first property on left, turn right at stile to climb path and steps between paddocks to enter hilltop playing field by kissing-gate. Follow left-hand side to leave at bottom corner and within 10 yards turn right down short path leading to road and back to start.

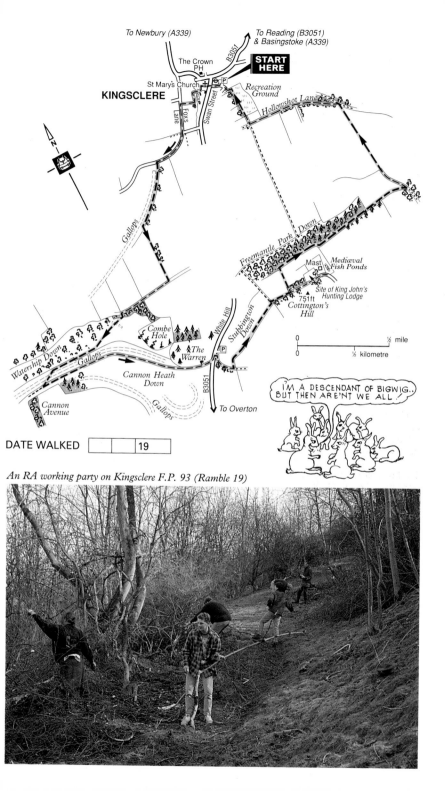

To Newbury (A339)

To Reading (B3051)
& Basingstoke (A339)

B3051

START HERE

The Crown PH

St Mary's Church

KINGSCLERE

Recreation Ground

Hollowshot Lane

Foxs Lane

Swan Street

N

Gallops

Freemantle Park Down

Mast

Mediæval Fish Ponds

Site of King John's Hunting Lodge

751ft
Cottington's Hill

Watership Down

Combe Hole

The Warren

White Hill

Stubbington Down

Gallops

Cannon Heath Down

Cannon Avenue

Gallops

B3051

To Overton

0   ½ mile
0   ½ kilometre

DATE WALKED   19

I'M A DESCENDANT OF BIGWIG..
BUT THEN ARE'NT WE ALL!

An RA working party on Kingsclere F.P. 93 (Ramble 19)

Hollowshot Lane and Hannington Village

Are you strong in wind and limb? This is not so much a walk, more a yomp, over the high chalk of the North Hampshire Downs, with plenty of 'ups'! Big fields, great skies, wide views. Share the scenery enjoyed by Roman centurions. March this way...

Distance: 6 or 4 miles
OS Map: Pathfinder 1203 Kingsclere
Start: Free public car park off Swan
            Street, Kingsclere (Grid ref:
            525586)

From entrance to car park turn sharp left up hill (Anchor Road). Follow left-hand footway straight on up, through metal barrier, and at top turn left into playing-field. Take a line half-right across field to gap in hedge. Follow this enclosed path, with houses below in old quarry, and at end bear right into broad hedged track, which bears left where downs come into view. At top of long steady climb, continue ahead on road round bend (Rectory Lane) and go straight on past buildings of Plantation Farm on concrete track, soon becoming gravel. Where track divides, bear left towards tree. (For shorter loop bear right - see map.) Track soon descends, crossing course of Portway, an early Roman road from Silchester to Salisbury, built for military purposes.

At bottom of slope cross road and climb wide track ahead, to left of Dutch barn, enjoying the switchback of hills, rolling like a gentle sea on all sides. Reaching path junction at top of Downs prepare to turn right but first, a short detour ahead, to end of copse, will provide good views on a clear day towards Overton and Basingstoke. Back at path junction take the path as mentioned, between open fields again. At T-junction turn left, alongside playing-field (Michaels Field) and then, facing Bertha's pretty cottage, turn right along lane to reach the manicured village green of Hannington, which has slumbered on this hilltop site since Saxon times.

The dainty well-head, prompted perhaps by its equally Victorian bigger brother on All Saints church, was built in 1897 to celebrate the Queen's Diamond Jubilee. The church itself enshrines the craftsmanship of a thousand years. Don't miss the solid Georgian facade of Dickers Farm, discreetly hidden behind its high yew hedges.

Having savoured these delights (including, perhaps, the 'Vine' pub, just along the road south of the green), follow drive to right of lych-gate and in front of gates ahead, turn right on path leading round

Cottington's Hill from Hollowshot Lane

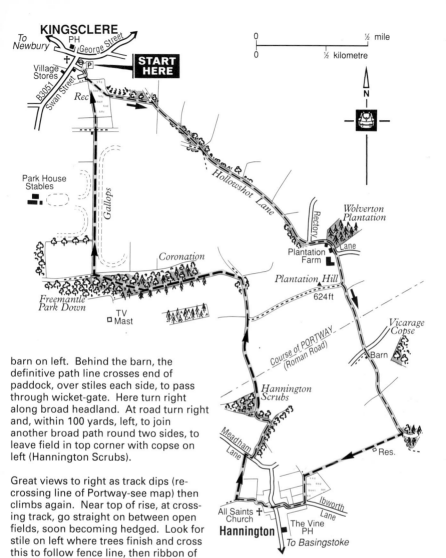

barn on left. Behind the barn, the definitive path line crosses end of paddock, over stiles each side, to pass through wicket-gate. Here turn right along broad headland. At road turn right and, within 100 yards, left, to join another broad path round two sides, to leave field in top corner with copse on left (Hannington Scrubs).

Great views to right as track dips (re-crossing line of Portway-see map) then climbs again. Near top of rise, at crossing track, go straight on between open fields, soon becoming hedged. Look for stile on left where trees finish and cross this to follow fence line, then ribbon of pines on left-hand boundary. Continue into plantation (Coronation) and look carefully for wide gap in trees to take right fork and gradually descend hillside on terraced path.

At bottom of slope bear left for 50 yards, then turn right over bank and leave woodland, to follow edge of gallops with hedge on left.

Generations of racehorses have been trained on the gallops around Kingsclere and up on the Downs, including six Derby winners at the end of last century. In recent years the most famous horse here has been 'Mill Reef'. Today, trainer

Ian Balding has around 100 thoroughbreds in his yard at Park House, including horses of HM The Queen and The Queen Mother.

At end of field cross track and stile ahead, to climb path and steps to re-enter playing-field. Follow left-hand side to leave at bottom corner and within 10 yards turn right down slope to estate road leading back to start.

Note: On this 6-mile circuit you have climbed up - and down - a total of 700 ft. Well done. Want to go round again?

DATE WALKED | | | 19 |

Plastow Green and Cheam School

An easy-going amble through quiet fields and hamlets with distant views to the Downs beyond Kingsclere. The only noisy spot may be the playing-fields of Cheam School, the well-known boys' preparatory school. The nine-year old heir to the Throne was here on 26 July 1958 when HM The Queen announced: "I intend to create my son, Charles, Prince of Wales today". Cream buns all round!

Distance: 5 miles
OS Map: Pathfinder 1187 Newbury
Start: Lay-by at Pitchorn Farm on A339, 6 miles SE of Newbury; 1½ miles N of Kingsclere. (Grid ref: 518606)

Facing large farm building, walk 40 paces to left of it, then turn right through metal gate and along broad farm track with hedge and field on left. Keep left of strip of water and from gateway marking end of first field, where track bears right between scattered trees, MAINTAIN SAME LINE STRAIGHT AHEAD across end of field, to reach single-plank bridge in far hedgerow. (Look back from time to time to check alignment.) In next field follow left-hand edge to end of copse, then turn left for 50 yards. Here cross stile on left into adjoining field and follow wide grass headland with hedge on right. At end of small copse, path dips back to right, soon becoming slightly sunken and tree-lined, before emerging by gate at roadside (Union Lane).

Bear right across road and up track past 'Copse Brook'. Cross culvert over stream and turn left, aiming for tall tree in top right-hand field corner, to continue along top of next field with hedge on left. At metal gate the right of way turns left, round two sides of paddocks ahead, to exit in far corner. Then, keeping to right of property, follow hedge on left through two more fields to enter fenced path, becoming sunken hedged track. Just beyond modern house (Summershurst Farm) bear right along field headland. At T-junction (Scarlett's Farm), turn left along drive which soon bears right into narrow lane between cottages of Plastow Green.

At road junction, facing 'Fairview', turn left. Pass drive to Hill House and at bottom of slope bear right over stile, to follow path across meadow, then footbridge (Kingsclere Brook - a great spot for snowdrops in season), finally along enclosed field-edge leading to road (Galley Lane). Turn right and follow road until, just beyond 'White House', turn left at end of conifers. Cross footbridge, then IMMEDIATELY turn right over same ditch. At end of enclosed path turn left over ditch and continue as before through narrow field to reach road (A339) opposite Cheam School. Cross carefully, turning left along verge. After stile into field on right keep along right-hand edge. Stay on same line alongside playing-field ahead, with good view of school to right. Still in playing-field, aim for left end of copse ahead. Pass through metal swing-gate to left of field corner and follow path alongside copse and over stile into woodland. Within a few yards, at end of bank, path bears right, goes down slope and over Ecchinswell Brook to enter field ahead. Here turn left, aiming for stile in right-hand fence ahead. Cross next field, towards buildings (Hyde Farm), followed by two more stiles and a long hedgerow on left to reach track at field end.

Now turn left, past small bungalow, and shortly left again into farm gateway, then immediately right, past thatched store, to enter field ahead. Stay on mid-field line through two fields, directly towards TV mast on horizon. Cross corner of copse and then keep left round boggy patch to reach stile, then concrete footbridge. Keep left of large field ahead and go straight on to cross single-plank bridge by largest tree near field corner.

Go ahead up bank, then through shrubbery, to follow right of way along left side of lawned area between bungalows. At end of grass use circular stepping stones in border leading to red-brick drive. Turn left along nursery access roadway and left again at main road, crossing carefully to return to start.

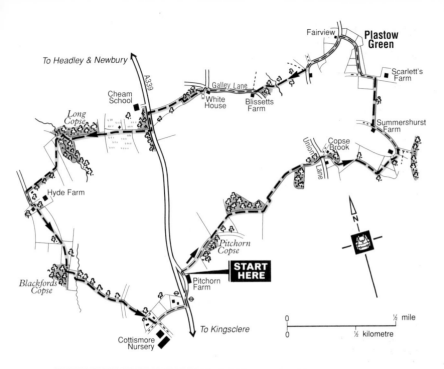

To Headley & Newbury

A339

Cheam School

Long Copse

Galley Lane

White House

Blissetts Farm

Fairview

Plastow Green

Scarlett's Farm

Summershurst Farm

Hyde Farm

Copse Brook

Union Lane

Blackfords Copse

Pitchorn Copse

START HERE

Pitchorn Farm

Cottismore Nursery

To Kingsclere

N

0   ½ mile
0   ½ kilometre

*Cheam School
from the footpath*

River Enborne and Huntsmoor Hill

A little dipper of a walk, up and down gentle slopes of the Enborne Valley, straddling the Berkshire/Hampshire border, between the modest heights of Crookham in the north and Huntsmoor Hill in the south.

Distance: 6¼ or 3½ miles
OS Map: Pathfinder 1187 Newbury
Start: 'Travellers Friend', Crookham (Grid ref: 537643) - where walkers are welcome to park. Pub is 2 miles SE of Thatcham BR Station

With your back to the 'Travellers Friend' turn right along road-side grass strip for some 85 yards, then cross over to enter drive between pillars (a right of way). Pass two properties on right and soon merge with track from left, sweeping gently down between open fields with distant views ahead. Follow track down through copse until, just before derelict cottage ahead, bear right through trees to reach field edge. The path line here lies straight ahead across three fields, almost touching left end of copse, finally to cross footbridge over River Enborne and so into Hampshire.

For a shorter alternative (3½ miles) turn left at this point - see map.

For the full circuit, turn sharp right after footbridge and follow wire fence on right, soon to cross stile leading to grass ribbon between river and field. Now follow river - the County boundary - for about a mile, to reach a ford.

At the ford, turn left up lane (Thorn Ford Lane) and at 'Maythorne' left again, along drive towards Folly Farm. At end of first field on right, turn right, a path now diverted round two sides of the next field. Just before end of hedge on second side, turn right into path enclosed between hedges, leading to front of modern house, 'Oakmoor', and follow drive to road.

Here turn right and shortly left along Common Road. Look for entrance on left to Kingsbrook House and a few yards down drive cross stile on right and follow left-hand side of field down to

cross footbridge (Kingsclere Brook) in bottom corner. Now turn right to follow field-edge to pass through swing-gate tucked away in top corner. Follow path through copse to find ahead an unexpected flight of rustic steps and bench seat adorning this side of Huntsmoor Hill.

The right of way goes straight up the hill before turning left along fence at top but you may prefer to turn left at foot of steps and at top of climb follow fence on right. At metal gate (leading to Hill House) turn left on broad track, becoming a gently descending bridleway leading to hamlet of Goose Hill. When level with first building on left (stable), turn right to enter narrow path to left of modern property, then follow drive and carefully cross road into broad track (Park Lane) which presently continues along right-hand side of field, then straight on into woodland. At end of woodland strip, emerging into field, go diagonally (almost a right-engle) towards power-line pole in far corner, to recross the patient Enborne at Park Gully Bridge.

Start to follow tarmac track then, by pair of oaks, bear right on line bisecting this corner of large field, to reach way-mark post on far side. From this point bear left, passing just left of tennis court and to right of house. Path continues to right of conifers before turning right (short length of 'permitted path') between garden fences. At lane turn left, then fork left to T-junction. Cross road ahead, go through swing-gate and over paddocks, aiming to left of cream-painted house (Stone House). Cross stile in corner and turn left along track to road. Cross road and turn right along grass verge at first, shortly to pass Manor Farm. Hopefully, the earlier pleasures of this walk will more than compensate for the few minutes of road walking back to the start, perhaps for some well-earned refreshment.

...... *sweeping gently down between open fields with distant views ahead*

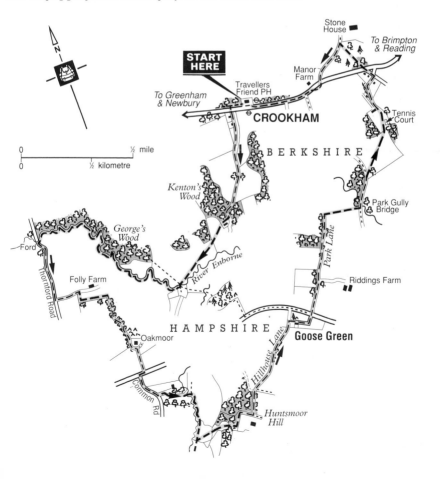

Stone House

To Brimpton & Reading

START HERE

Manor Farm

Travellers Friend PH

To Greenham & Newbury

CROOKHAM

Tennis Court

BERKSHIRE

Kenton's Wood

Park Gully Bridge

George's Wood

Ford

River Enborne

Park Lane

Thornford Road

Folly Farm

Riddings Farm

HAMPSHIRE

Oakmoor

Goose Green

Hillhouse Lane

Common Rd

Huntsmoor Hill

½ mile

½ kilometre

Little Park Farm
and Inwood Copse

Ramble 22

A short train or bus ride (from
Woolhampton to Thatcham) makes up
the third side of this undemanding stroll
to Ashford Hill through the quiet river
valleys of the Kennet and Enborne. Ride
before or after the walk, whichever best
suits the limited timetable. With a little
planning the car could even be left at
home.

Distance: 7 miles
OS Map: Pathfinder 1187 Newbury
Start: Thatcham BR Station (Grid ref:
         528664). If you miss the train
         back, a 3-mile length of canal
         towpath links the two stations
         - see map.

From Thatcham Station cross bridge
over canal and River Kennet and shortly
bear left along lane to pass
Chamberhouse Mill. At fork, bear left of
'Crookham Willows', along narrow drive,
hedged at first, then with Kennet nearby
on left. Until diverted recently, this right
of way went straight between buildings
ahead (it was a farm, never a manor-
house).

So now, in sight of house ahead, turn
right over stile and weave your way
between buildings and stream.
Reaching white-painted store, turn right
to pass tennis court and along headland
track with hedge on right. Just 30 yards
after bend in track, turn right into
woodland path, open at first with new
planting, then climb steadily with high
wire fence nearby on left. At top of slope
continue on concrete roadway (built as
access to war-time USAF 'Flying
Fortress' bomb-store) and pass
Crookham Park to reach road junction at
Crookham Common.

Turn left along road for 25 yards, then
bear left along woodland strip. Cross
road at 'Travellers Friend' and follow
right-hand verge through Crookham village until, opposite entrance to Manor
Farm, turn right along hedged drive
(signed 'Little Park Farm'). Admire
immaculate lawns and hedges of Park
Field on left. After cottages/barn of Little
Park Farm drive descends, with fine
views through trees to Watership Down.
Cross Park Gully bridge (into Hampshire)

and turn left along bank of River
Enborne. At end of first field cross ditch
and follow right-hand headland of next
field, with wood on right. At corner of
field turn right into trees, on wide grass
track. Emerging at field edge, bear left
alongside headland and after 100 yards
cross plank-bridge and continue uphill
close to edge of big field. At lane turn
right until, just before top of slope, bear
left onto gravel track, which continues
after cottages as grass path between
hedges. After cottage on left, path joins
track leading to Ashford Hill.

See map to visit shop, pub, nature
reserve, etc. close by on right.

To continue, where track bends right,
keep straight on to pass Brook Farm.
Cross stile by metal gate and go slightly
left across meadow, through gap into
next field and follow hedge on right.
After plank-bridge across gully, maintain
same direction and cross bridge/stile
into next field, soon following woodland
on right, finally leaving fields by metal
gate. Within 50 yards cross lane and go
straight ahead into Inwood Copse.

Path ahead leads to new footbridge over
the Enborne, a 'missing link' across the
county boundary for decades. (A local
story recalls that a former owner of Hyde
End Farm - a mining engineer - blew up
the old bridge many years ago to facilitate his duck-shoot!) After the bridge go
straight on through two meadows, aiming between tree clump and river (a
glimpse of Brimpton Church spire on
horizon to left). Exit second meadow
and bear half-right in next field, keeping
some five yards from hedge at first, then
continue on same line to cross

THATCHAM

footbridge on far side. Turn right on farm track until, within a few yards of road, turn sharp left up towards Heaven and St Peter's Church (built 1870).

Take path through churchyard, down slope to war memorial and turn right along road. Shortly, cross road opposite shop and stay on that side before bearing left, signed: 'Aldermaston'. Ten yards past Brimpton Lodge turn left down side of Glebe Cottage into hedged path at first, then straight on along gravel track. (A Roman road crossed this track but the flat scenery owes more to gravel extraction.) Bear left at fork and reaching trees at end of fields turn right, leading to road. Turn left past the canal-side 'Rowbarge' Inn and within a few yards reach Midgham Station. (It is said that it was not called Woolhampton to avoid possible confusion with Wolverhampton!)

DATE WALKED		19

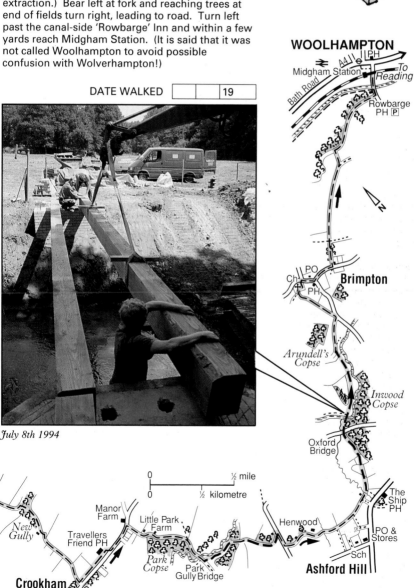

July 8th 1994

WOOLHAMPTON

Wasing Church and Hyde End

Explore the hills, woods and unspoilt water-meadows straddling the Enborne Valley and the Berkshire/Hampshire border. There are five church spires to be seen on hilltop sites - Brimpton, Aldermaston, Wasing, Midgham and Ashford Hill. But which three are identical, designed by the same architect?* A truly inspiring walk!

Distance: 6½ miles
OS Map: Pathfinder 1187 Newbury
Start: Verge parking opposite The Pineapple inn on B3051 at Brimpton Common, 1½ miles SE of Brimpton village. (Grid ref: 567629)

Take the path directly opposite 'Pineapple' and follow this through paddock. Carefully cross road and continue ahead along byway. Where track turn left at grass triangle, go straight on along footpath, soon passing 'Woodside' to T-junction (Wasing Wood). Turn left along edge of wood. Beyond house the track is a 'permitted path' until reaching a way-mark post where a right of way joins from left. Here go straight on, following row of old yews. Path becomes hedged, then fenced through parkland and mansion of Wasing Place comes into view. The house we see was largely rebuilt in 1945, after a fire, to resemble the original Adam-style building of 1773. Reaching broad crossing track (leading to farm buildings on left) go straight on, through squeeze-stile beside paddock fence. At corner of field cross tarmac drive to enter churchyard just ahead, through white gates.

St Nicholas's Church was largely rebuilt in 1761 but retains many earlier features, including 13th century lancet windows in the chancel and a fascinating list of past incumbents and Lords of the Manor.

Returning to drive, turn right and follow it down through park to Lodge. Here turn left and immediately right over Shalford Bridge (and the Enborne). Take left fork in road and, where this bends left, pass to left of metal gate and take footpath along edge of gravel workings. At end of large open field on right, turn

left into hedged path to reach road by Glebe Cottage. Turn right for 25 yards, then left through swing-gate. Half-way up left side of field cross stile and continue in same direction, to leave field by narrow path between two pairs of houses. Follow road through estate and cross at junction to reach entrance to St Peter's Almshouses. Turn right and follow footway round past 'Three Horse Shoes'. At war memorial turn left up gravel drive to St Peter's Church (1870), the focal point of Brimpton.

Enter walled path to left of churchyard, then go straight on along headland with hedge on right for several hundred yards before bearing left onto grass strip linking power-line poles. Path continues between paddocks to reach road. Turn left down road (not sharp left), soon becoming gravel, to pass on left Hyde End House. As track swings left, cross stile ahead, where the right of way now follows the Enborne riverbank. Cross this field to neck of land between pond on left and river - this was once a trout farm. Follow riverbank in next field to reach and turn right over new footbridge (into Hampshire), installed by Berkshire County Council at our request in July 1994, a 'missing link' in the footpath network for decades. (See note in Ramble 22.) Follow woodland path (Inwood Copse), cross lane, then straight on past metal gate ahead and along top of field. Cross stile/footbridge into next field, go diagonally downhill using plank-bridge over gully and through gateway, with village houses in view. Keep left of oak tree in bottom corner so as to cross stile into water-meadow (SSSI). Cross meadow to stile at road, close to the 'Ship'. Turn right and immediately left after bridge, to enter Ashford Hill Nature Reserve, a treasure-trove of marshland plants and insects (more details in Ramble 24).

Enter meadows and follow left-hand ditch of first field (Piper's Piece) to find in corner concrete 'squeeze-bridge'. Continue, again keeping to left, this time to pass through swing-gate. Now head diagonally in similar direction, aiming for left-hand end of trees on hillside ahead. Enter woodland (Redland Copse).

To A4, Thatcham & Newbury

BRIMPTON
St Peter's Church
PO & Stores
Glebe Cottage
PH

R. Enborne
Shalford Bridge
Wasing Park

St Nicholas's Church
Wasing Farm

Village Hall

BERKSHIRE

Hyde End

Wasing Wood

N

Inwood Copse

P

START HERE

Brimpton Common
B3051

A340 to Tadley & Basingstoke

The Pineapple PH

HAMPSHIRE

SSSI
Brook Farm
Ship PH

Ashford Hill

Ashford Hill Meadows
(Nature Reserve)

0   ½ mile
0   ½ kilometre

DATE WALKED | | | 19

at stile in corner and climb steadily through woods until, at top, enter field on left at clear opening. Now aim towards left-hand end of distant houses but just beyond far field boundary, at tall pine tree, turn left along path over gorse and bracken covered common. At T-junction turn left along track to road and, shortly ahead, the inviting 'Pineapple'.

* Brimpton, Midgham & Ashford Hill

Traditional grazing, Ashford Hill Meadows

Baughurst and Ashford Hill Meadows

Trees and more trees; cool in summer, sheltered in winter, beautiful at all times. A necklace of woodland copses, clasped together by a superb National Nature Reserve, sometimes grazed by shaggy Highland cattle. What's keeping you?

Distance: 5 miles
OS Map: Pathfinder 1187 Newbury
Start: Heath End village hall car
           park, Baughurst, near Tadley
           (Grid ref: 581621)

From car park pass between posts to left of hall and then diagonally over grass area to cross road (Bishopwood Lane). Go straight along gravel track ahead, between gardens at first, then along woodland strip, finally emerging on broad track leading to road (Baughurst Road). Cross over, turning left and between last house, 'Downsview', and former Methodist Chapel (1872), turn right into bridleway. Shortly, at end of field behind chapel, turn left through gate and along field-edge path. Look for power-line pole ahead and from this point cross field towards red-brick house, with good views on right towards Watership Down.

Immediately in front of house turn right on path between bushes and low banks. Pass through old metal gate and bear left into field opening, to follow left-hand hedgerow round two sides before crossing plank bridge in far corner. Continue in next field with hedge again on left. At entrance to adjoining field go slightly right to find footbridge and stile tucked away in corner. A line just to left through middle of field ahead brings you to stile at road.

Turn right on road (Violet Lane) then immediately left at fork, soon passing Meadow Cottage. Where tarmac surface ends continue on rough roadway until, when level with end of field on right, turn left over stile to follow right-hand side of field, with path at times in trees (the path may have been originally in the gully here). At end of field turn right along track and cross culvert to reach stile by metal gates. Turn right along lane, past 'Snowdrop Cottage', and at

junction right again for a few yards before turning left up gravel track at side of houses and along edge of woodland (Smithleys Copse). Where field on left ends, don't turn left but keep to right side of clear strip ahead, going downhill until, just before bottom of slope, turn right into trees to arrive at bridge over Sandford Stream.

After bridge, turn left for a few yards then right, up bank. Follow path ahead, ignoring others, until at T-junction, facing woods, turn left on path between deep ditches. At end of field on left, turn right onto broad grass ride, dividing Butlers from Sleepers Copse. Stay on main ride until grass ends, then bear left and right to reach swing-gate marking entrance to Ashford Hill Meadows - a National Nature Reserve, managed by English Nature.

This 50-acre paradise for naturalists is a rare survivor of traditional style water-meadow farming, managed for many years by hay-making and grazing, with little or no fertiliser. 235 plant species, 32 species of butterfly and over 360 types of moth have been recorded in the reserve.

Go ahead across water-meadow (field-name 'Sleepers') towards foot-bridge, which do not cross but turn right alongside stream (Baughurst Brook) and over stile at end of field. Cross footbridge and bear left beside brook on path which shortly rises to go diagonally across field and straight into woodland, just a few yards right of field corner (Great Haughurst Wood). At fork go left down slope and over footbridge, turn right for a few yards before ascending to emerge from woods. Turn left through store-yard to road. Here turn right and opposite first property turn left into bridleway, leading through woodland to road (Brimpton Road). Cross ahead into estate path, turn right at garages and then left into Wellington Crescent and so back to start.

DATE WALKED [   ]